KT-119-085

Contents

The night sky

When you look up
at the sky on a
clear night, you are
looking into Space.

Millions of stars
twinkle in the
darkness, but the
Moon looks much
brighter than
any star. It is the
brightest object
in the sky.

The Moon
looks big in
the night sky.

STARTERS

The Moon

Claire Llewellyn

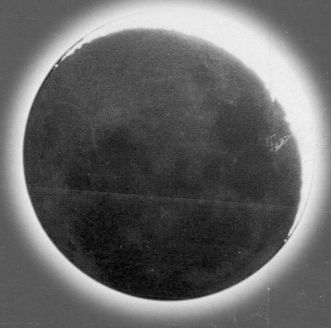

Text copyright © Claire Llewellyn 2003

Science consultant: Dr Carol Ballard
Language consultant: Andrew Burrell
Design: Perry Tate Design

Published in Great Britain in 2003
by Hodder Wayland, an imprint of
Hodder Children's Books

This paperback edition published in 2008 by Wayland,
a division of Hachette Children's Books, an Hachette Livre UK company.

The publishers would like to thank the following for allowing us to reproduce their
pictures in this book: Science Photo Library; title page, contents page, 6-9, 11, 15-18
(top), 19, 22, 24 (bottom 3 pictures) / Bruce Coleman; cover, 5, 10, 12-14 / Genesis;
18 (right), 21, 24 (top) / Galaxy Pictures; 23

A Catalogue record for this book is available from the British Library.

ISBN: 978 0 7502 4284 4

Printed and bound in China

Wayland
A division of Hachette Children's Books
338 Euston Road, London NW1 3BH

Earth's neighbour

We live on a planet called Earth, a giant rocky ball that spins in Space. The Moon is our nearest neighbour.

The Earth is four times bigger than the Moon.

But the Moon is still a long way away. If you could drive a car to the Moon, it would take more than half a year!

A rocket takes three days to get to the Moon.

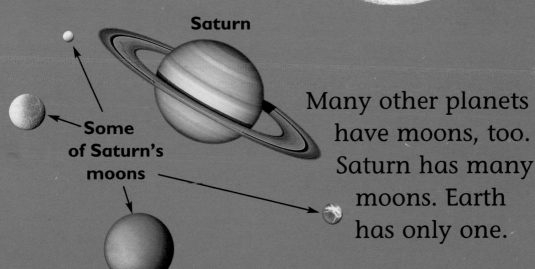

Saturn

Some of Saturn's moons

Many other planets have moons, too. Saturn has many moons. Earth has only one.

The Moon's orbit

The Moon is a rocky ball, just like the Earth, and it is always moving. It travels round and round the Earth, following a path called an orbit.

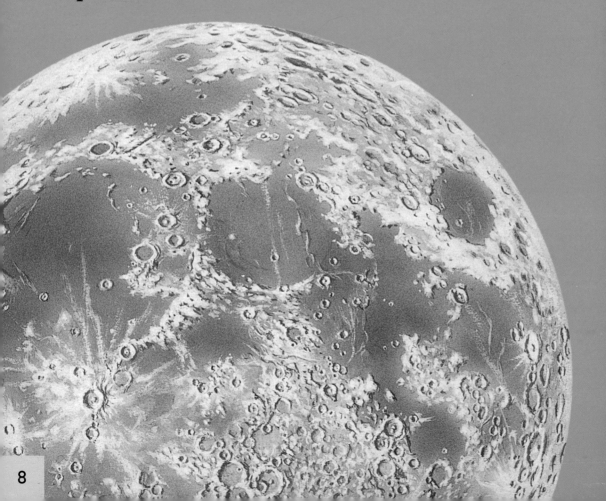

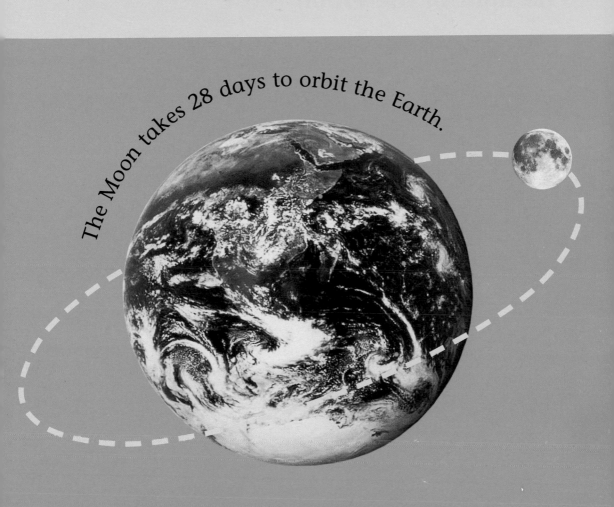

The Moon takes 28 days to orbit the Earth.

The Earth and the Moon belong to the solar system, a **BIG** family of planets and moons that travel around the Sun.

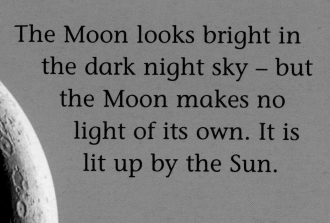

The Moon looks bright in the dark night sky – but the Moon makes no light of its own. It is lit up by the Sun.

We can only see the part of the Moon that is lit up by the Sun.

The Sun's light hits the Moon and bounces down to the Earth. To us, this light looks very pale. We call it moonlight.

Moonlight is soft
and silvery, but
on some nights it
helps us to see.

The shape of the Moon

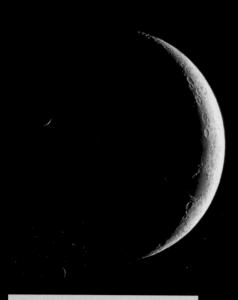

A crescent moon

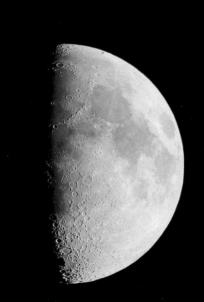

A half moon

A full moon

As the Moon travels around the Earth, its shape appears to change. Each night, it looks a little bit different from the way it looked the night before.

For 14 nights, the Moon seems to grow bigger and bigger until it is a huge round ball. Then, for 14 nights, it seems to grow smaller again until we see nothing at all.

Moon watching

If you use a telescope or binoculars, you can see the Moon's surface clearly.

The surface is covered with holes called craters, which are **wide** and very **deep**. They were made when huge rocks hurtled through Space, and crashed into the Moon.

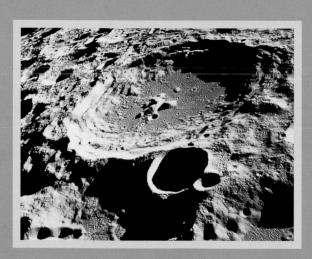

These dark patches are flat areas.

These light patches are rocky mountains.

On the Moon

There is no water or air on the Moon. There are no clouds, and no wind or rain. Nothing can grow or live there – not a single animal or plant.

By day, the Moon is boiling hot. By night, it's freezing cold.

The sky is always pitch black.

Going to the Moon

Astronauts have travelled to the Moon in rockets. They wore spacesuits to protect them from the heat and the cold, and to give them a supply of air.

The astronauts took a SMALLER spacecraft down to the Moon itself.

The Moon landings helped scientists to find out all sorts of things – such as how old the Moon is and how it was made.

The astronauts collected rocks for scientists to study.

Walking on the Moon

Walking on the Moon looks fun.
The astronauts could take **giant** steps
and bounce high off the ground.

On Earth, an invisible force called gravity keeps us on the ground. Gravity is not as **strong** on the Moon so people feel much lighter.

You weigh a lot less on the Moon.

You can jump a lot higher, too.

Leaving the Moon

The astronauts returned to
their rocket and travelled back
to Earth. They left behind a
flag and lots of footprints on
the surface.

You can see
the planet
Earth in this
picture of
the Moon.

We do not know when people will return to the Moon. Maybe one day, scientists will build a space station there and we will all be able to visit the Moon.

Glossary and index

Astronaut A scientist who travels into Space.

Crater A large round hole in the ground.

Gravity An invisible pulling force.

Moon A rocky ball that orbits a planet.

Orbit The path that a moon takes around a planet, or a planet takes around the Sun.

Planet A large ball that orbits the Sun.

Solar system All the planets and moons that move around the Sun.

Space Everything that lies beyond the Earth.

Spacecraft A vehicle used for space travel.

Star A ball of hot gas. We see stars shining in the night sky.